mighty machines

TRAINS

Written by
Adam Hibbert

Illustrated by
Stephen Angel

p

This is a Parragon Book
First published in 2001

Parragon
Queen Street House
4 Queen Street
Bath BA1 1HE, UK

Copyright © Parragon 2001

Produced by

David West ⚤ Children's Books
7 Princeton Court
55 Felsham Road
Putney
London SW15 1AZ

British Library Cataloguing-in-Publication Data

A catalogue record for this book is available from
the British Library.

ISBN 0-75254-678-3

Printed in U.A.E

Designers
Diane Clouting
Aarti Parmar
Illustrator
Stephen Angel
(SGA)
Cartoonist
Peter Wilks
(SGA)
Editor
James Pickering
Consultant
Steve Parker

CONTENTS

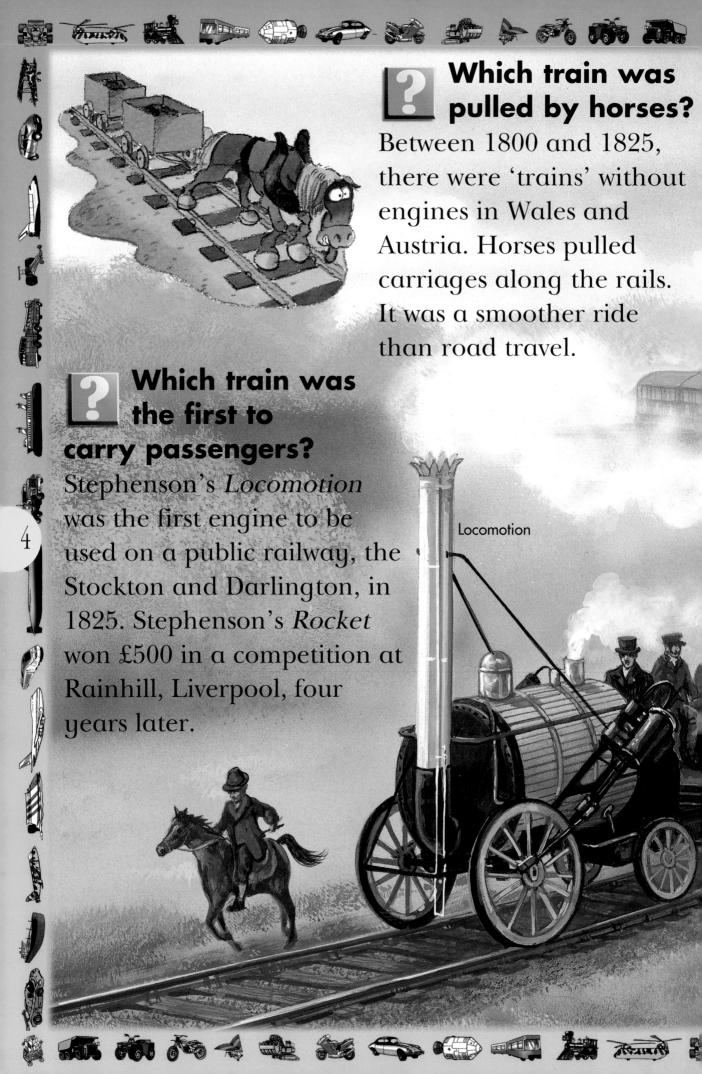

? Which train was pulled by horses?

Between 1800 and 1825, there were 'trains' without engines in Wales and Austria. Horses pulled carriages along the rails. It was a smoother ride than road travel.

? Which train was the first to carry passengers?

Stephenson's *Locomotion* was the first engine to be used on a public railway, the Stockton and Darlington, in 1825. Stephenson's *Rocket* won £500 in a competition at Rainhill, Liverpool, four years later.

Locomotion

Trevithick's "Catch Me Me Who Can', 1808

What was the first train engine?

Richard Trevithick, a mine engineer, first demonstrated a mobile engine on rails in 1804. It pulled 70 men and ten tonnes of iron ore, in front of a crowd of amazed onlookers. His next engine became a fairground ride.

Horse-drawn railway

Amazing! There were horse-drawn trains 50 years ago! The Fintona Branch of Ireland's Great Northern railway remained horse-powered until the early 1950s.

Is it true?
The ancient Greeks had a steam engine!

Yes. Hero of Alexander wrote about a steam-powered spinning ball, called the 'aeolipile' in 200 BC. But since slave labour was free, no one bothered to use the engine as a labour-saving device.

Couplings

? How do trains fit together?

Trains use special links called couplings to clip different parts together. Trains used to be coupled by hand, which could be dangerous.

American Baldwin locomotive

? What's a locomotive?

A locomotive is the part of the train which contains the engine. It does the work of pulling (or pushing) the train along the track. Locomotives may have to carry their fuel with them. They have special wheels to grip the track.

6

Who steers the train?

Junction box

Trains follow the track they're on, so they don't need a steering wheel. A person in the junction box can change the direction of a train by moving special junctions in the track called points.

Amazing! Some trains lean over! Modern fast trains take corners so quickly that passengers might slosh around inside. Computers in the train 'feel' the sideways forces, and tilt the train in the other direction so that you don't spill your tea.

7

Is it true?
Some trains are blown along by the wind.

Yes. At least, some were, especially when fuel was hard to find. America's Baltimore & Ohio railroad experimented with sail power in the 1830s.

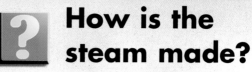

Boiler

Smoke stack

Piston

? How does steam power work?

A steam engine is like a big kettle. It uses the pressure of steam to push against pistons inside cylinders. The pistons move sliding rods called linkages, which turn the wheels and make the train move.

? How is the steam made?

Steam trains all need a fireperson, who shovels coal, or similar fuel, into a firebox. The heat of the fire boils the water, which turns to steam. Smoke from the fire puffs out of the funnel on the smoke stack.

Russian royal railway, 1837

Amazing! Russia's first railway was just for royal holidays! The Tsar of Russia had three locomotives made for him in 1837. They ran on a private line from his palace to a royal resort.

8

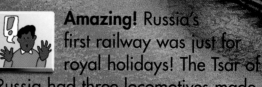

Steam trains could do 200 kph.

Yes. In 1938, a steam engine called *Mallard* reached 202.7 kph, while pulling a 240 tonne train. That's still a record for a steam engine. It had been souped-up by Herbert Gresley, doubling its power. *Mallard* is now in a museum in York.

When was steam power used?

The golden age of steam was from about 1850, until as late as 1950. Since then, steam trains have disappeared from industrial countries, where they only survive as tourist attractions. Steam locomotives still do most of the hard work in many developing countries.

Patrick Stirling's
Single locomotive

9

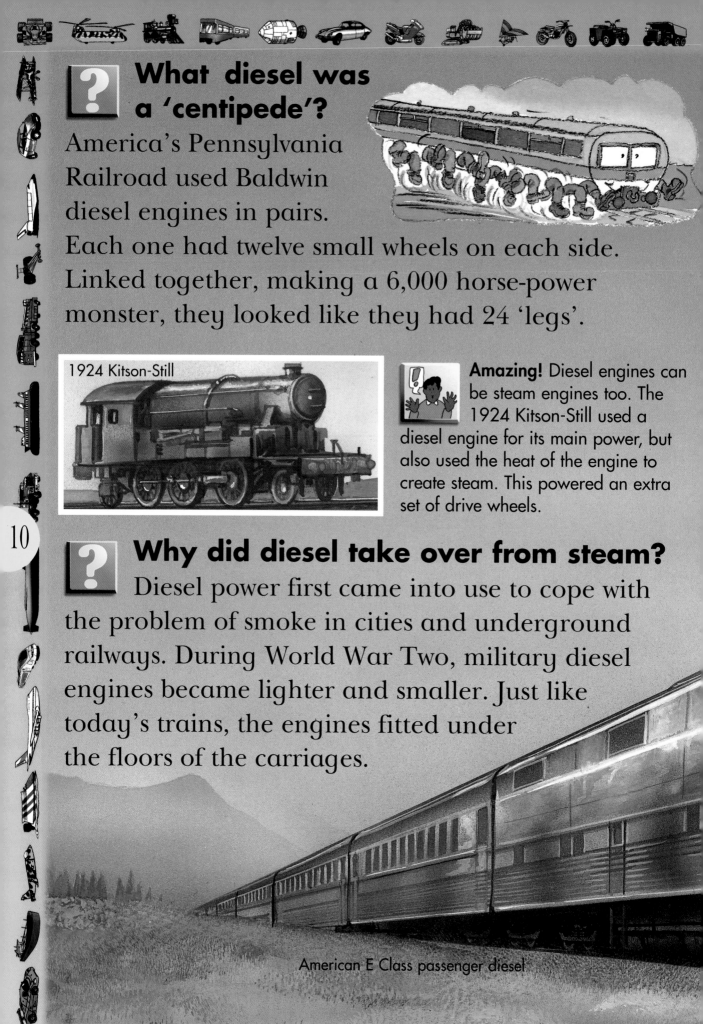

? What diesel was a 'centipede'?

America's Pennsylvania Railroad used Baldwin diesel engines in pairs. Each one had twelve small wheels on each side. Linked together, making a 6,000 horse-power monster, they looked like they had 24 'legs'.

1924 Kitson-Still

Amazing! Diesel engines can be steam engines too. The 1924 Kitson-Still used a diesel engine for its main power, but also used the heat of the engine to create steam. This powered an extra set of drive wheels.

? Why did diesel take over from steam?

Diesel power first came into use to cope with the problem of smoke in cities and underground railways. During World War Two, military diesel engines became lighter and smaller. Just like today's trains, the engines fitted under the floors of the carriages.

American E Class passenger diesel

Which diesel looked like an aeroplane?

1931 Kruckenburg

The German Kruckenburg of 1931 had a huge propeller at the back which pushed it along like an aeroplane on rails. It reached speeds up to 230 kph during a ten-kilometre speed trial. Unfortunately, it was too noisy and dangerous for everyday use.

Is it true?
Diesel engines use electric motors.

Yes. Many diesel-engined trains actually use electric motors to turn the wheels. The engine itself uses diesel fuel. It turns a generator, which creates the electricity needed by the electric motors. This is because electric motors turn powerfully at all speeds, unlike a diesel engine.

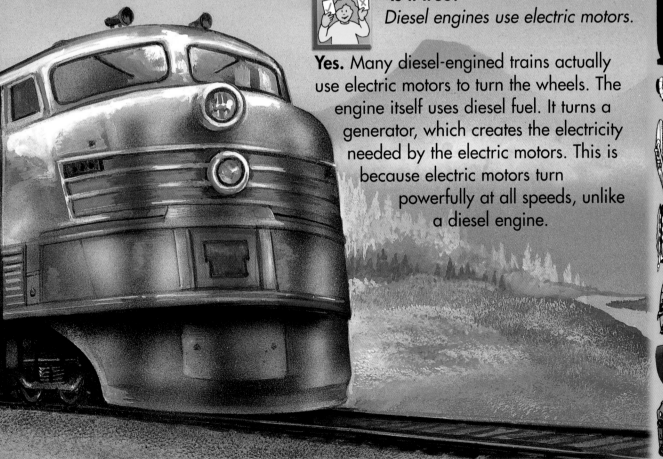

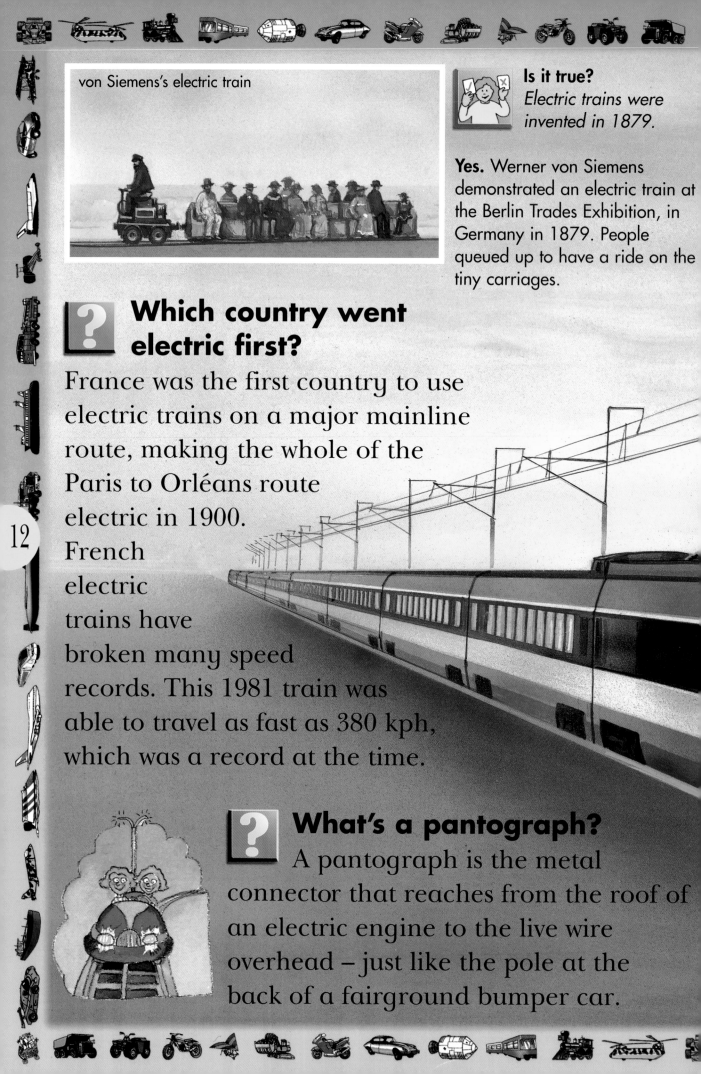

von Siemens's electric train

Is it true?
Electric trains were invented in 1879.

Yes. Werner von Siemens demonstrated an electric train at the Berlin Trades Exhibition, in Germany in 1879. People queued up to have a ride on the tiny carriages.

? Which country went electric first?

France was the first country to use electric trains on a major mainline route, making the whole of the Paris to Orléans route electric in 1900. French electric trains have broken many speed records. This 1981 train was able to travel as fast as 380 kph, which was a record at the time.

12

? What's a pantograph?

A pantograph is the metal connector that reaches from the roof of an electric engine to the live wire overhead — just like the pole at the back of a fairground bumper car.

Amazing! One electric train travels all over Europe. Trans-Europ-Express was designed to use the different electricity supplies in different European countries. Engineers have to change its wheels though, every time it travels in and out of Spain.

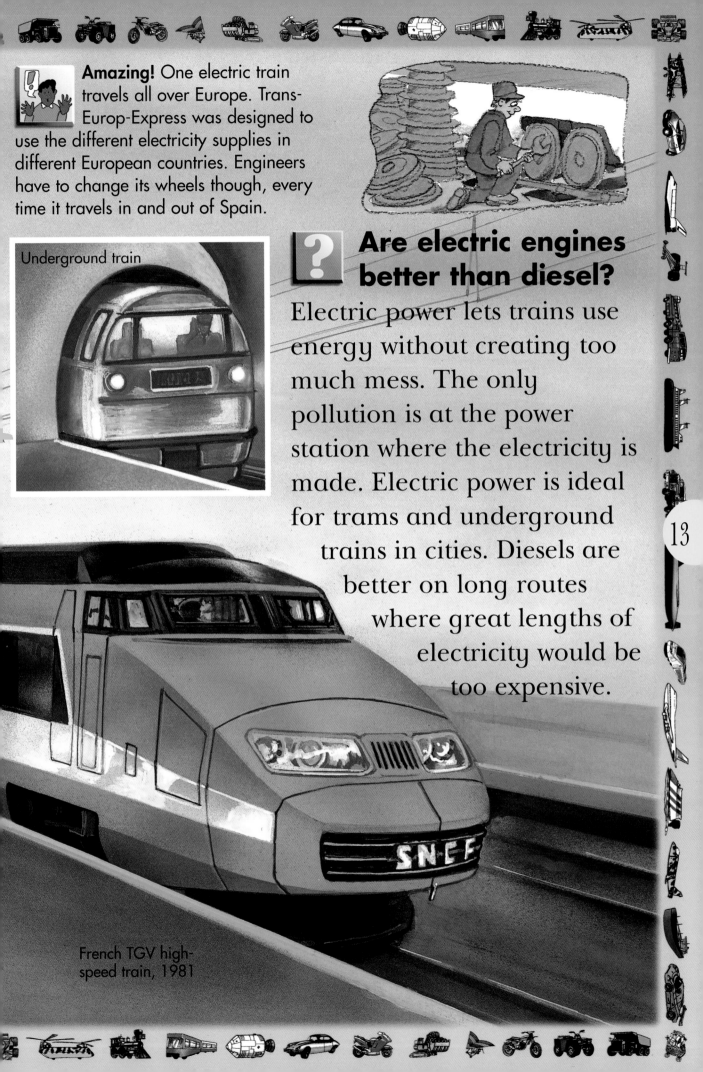

Underground train

? Are electric engines better than diesel?

Electric power lets trains use energy without creating too much mess. The only pollution is at the power station where the electricity is made. Electric power is ideal for trams and underground trains in cities. Diesels are better on long routes where great lengths of electricity would be too expensive.

13

French TGV high-speed train, 1981

British Rail coal train

❓ What is a chaldron?

Coal wagons are also called chaldrons. They are loaded at the mine, then travel to the nearest port for loading on to boats, or to a power station. Chaldrons are emptied by tipping them over, or by opening a trapdoor below.

Dining car in the Orient Express

❓ Which train was the most luxurious?

The Orient Express offered passengers a lounge, a ladies' drawing room, fully-serviced bedroom suites, and a fantastic dining room. Diners ate in evening dress. A modern version of the Orient Express still runs between London and Venice.

14

Amazing! Until the invention of the air brake in 1869, brakemen had to run along the train applying brakes in every car, one by one! Today the brakes are worked by the driver.

What's a Pullman?

George Pullman was a carpenter who repaired two tatty passenger carriages in Chicago in 1859. By the 1920s, the Pullman company had 10,000 luxurious Pullman cars in service. They became famous for the comfort, style and excellent service offered to their lucky passengers.

Mail train

15

Is it true?
There are post offices on wheels.

Yes. There are underground and overground mail trains all over the world. Some don't stop – instead, bags of mail are caught or dropped off as the train whizzes past. Sorters in the train work very quickly in case any of the collected mail has to go to the next station!

 Who rode on a wooden track?

Alpine rack and pinion railway

A seven-kilometre track in Tasmania was made of gum tree wood! Convicts pushed carts up a hill, then jumped aboard for the downhill ride.

Amazing! Some trains have teeth! On steep hills smooth track is too slippery. Trains would slip going up and slide on the way down! 'Rack and pinion' tracks have a third, toothed rail, for trains to grip with a special cog, or 'tooth', on the wheel.

16

How are tracks laid?

Firstly the ground must be prepared. This might mean clearing woodland, or cutting a flat route through hilly land. Wooden 'sleepers' are laid at exact distances from each other, and the metal rails are then attached to them. As the track gets longer, supply trains travel along it, delivering more sleepers and rails.

Sleeper

No. Monorails have just one. Monorail trains are important parts of the transport system in many big cities. Monorail systems are often found in amusement parks, airports and large industrial sites.

? Which train was pushed by air?

In 1861, a train was built which was pushed through a tunnel by a blast of air. The tunnel was only 76 centimetres wide, and the experimental train was designed to carry mail bags.

Monorail

17

Track-laying in Canada, 1880

Which trains travel by cables?

San Francisco cable car

Cable cars, such as the ones in San Francisco, are pulled along by a moving loop of cable, made from strong steel. The cable passes through a slot between the rails, and the cars fix on to it. This way, cable cars can climb very steep hills.

Where is the longest straight?

It's difficult to build straight stretches of track near towns, but much easier in empty parts of the world. The longest stretch of straight track is in the desert of Australia. It is perfectly straight for 478 kilometres.

SPARES

Amazing! Railways can go missing! During the American Civil War, the South ripped up some of its less important railways to use as spare parts along the battle front. The states of Florida and Texas gave up their entire networks!

18

Yes. If all the train track in America was laid end-to-end it would form a single track which would go almost six times around the world – that's 240,000 kilometres!

? Can trains travel the length of Africa?

There is no direct link from Cairo in North Africa to Cape Town, South Africa, 9,760 kilometres away. Cecil Rhodes tried to build a railway line in the late 19th century, but one of his problems was finding enough workmen. 28 of his men were eaten by lions on the Athi Plains in Kenya! However there are plans to complete this link soon.

Australian Indian Pacific railway

19

❓ Is the Channel Tunnel longest?

Not quite. The Channel Tunnel is 49.8 kilometres in total. The Seikan, Japan's tunnel between the main islands of Honshu and Hokkaido, travels an amazing 53.9 kilometres underground.

Tunnel-boring machine

❓ How do trains cross rivers?

Trains use big bridges or deep tunnels to cross the largest rivers. The Victorian engineer, Isambard Kingdom Brunel, invented strong metal bridges to carry the weight of a train. Some bridges are so big that repainting them is a full-time job!

Where was the first raised city railway?

New York City had a serious traffic problem in the 1880s, and that was before cars! An 'Elevated Railway', known as 'the L' for short, was built above the streets. It still works today.

New York Elevated Railway

Amazing! You can take a train on a boat. Train ferries started operating in the late 1800s between England and France. Passengers stayed in their seats all the way from London to Paris!

Is it true?
Box Hill tunnel knows its creator's birthday.

Yes. Brunel built it at a special angle. Each year, only on his birthday, the sun shines right through the entire 3.2 kilometre tunnel in southern England.

I.K.BRUNEL

Royal Albert Bridge, spanning the River Tamar, England

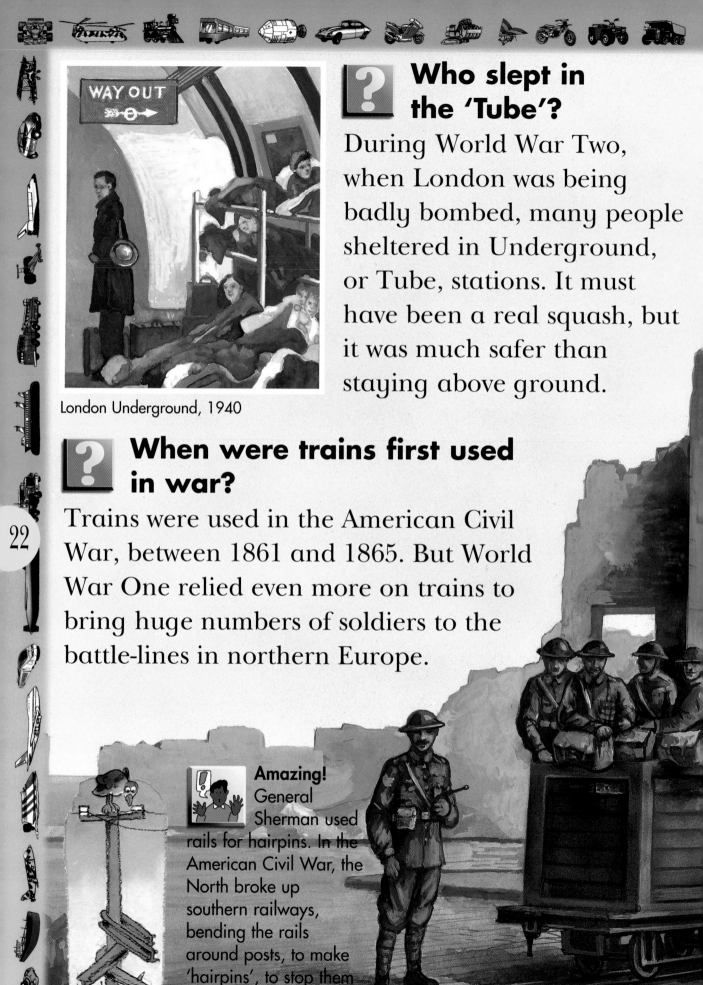

Who slept in the 'Tube'?

During World War Two, when London was being badly bombed, many people sheltered in Underground, or Tube, stations. It must have been a real squash, but it was much safer than staying above ground.

London Underground, 1940

When were trains first used in war?

Trains were used in the American Civil War, between 1861 and 1865. But World War One relied even more on trains to bring huge numbers of soldiers to the battle-lines in northern Europe.

Amazing! General Sherman used rails for hairpins. In the American Civil War, the North broke up southern railways, bending the rails around posts, to make 'hairpins', to stop them being reused.

Is it true?
The first tanks travelled by train.

Yes. In World War One, secret new tanks were wrapped up and shipped to battle by train. Everyone was told the bundles were oil tanks, and the name stuck!

Armoured train, South Africa, 1900

❓ What train is a tank?
Some trains were armoured, to protect important generals, as they travelled around with orders for their troops. Some armoured trains even had cannons on board!

World War One troop transporter

What was the biggest train crime?

In 1963 a train full of used banknotes was robbed in Buckinghamshire, England. The thieves got away with over £2.5 million, a huge sum of money even today.

Scene of the Great Train Robbery

Amazing! Trains at Mwatate Dam have to mind out for demons. The Kenyan villagers nearby, thought that trains were having a lot of accidents there because the local spirits were angry. Trains began pausing briefly to salute the spirits, and there hasn't been a crash since!

Do trains crash?

Trains occasionally crash for a number of reasons – there might be a points failure, or a weak bridge. Amazingly, no one was killed when this cattle train crashed through the front of an Irish railway station. Rail travel is usually very safe though.

Train crash, Harcourt Street Station, Dublin

Did railway projects always work?

No. The English almost built a Channel Tunnel in 1883. They tunnelled roughly two kilometres under the sea, but the government was worried the French would use the tunnel to invade England, so it was abandoned!

Is it true?
Some trains are too big.

Yes. The Soviet Union made a locomotive in 1934 that was too long. Its non-swivelling wheels and heavy weight actually straightened out curves in the track, leaving it stuck in a ditch!

Derailment, Russia 1934

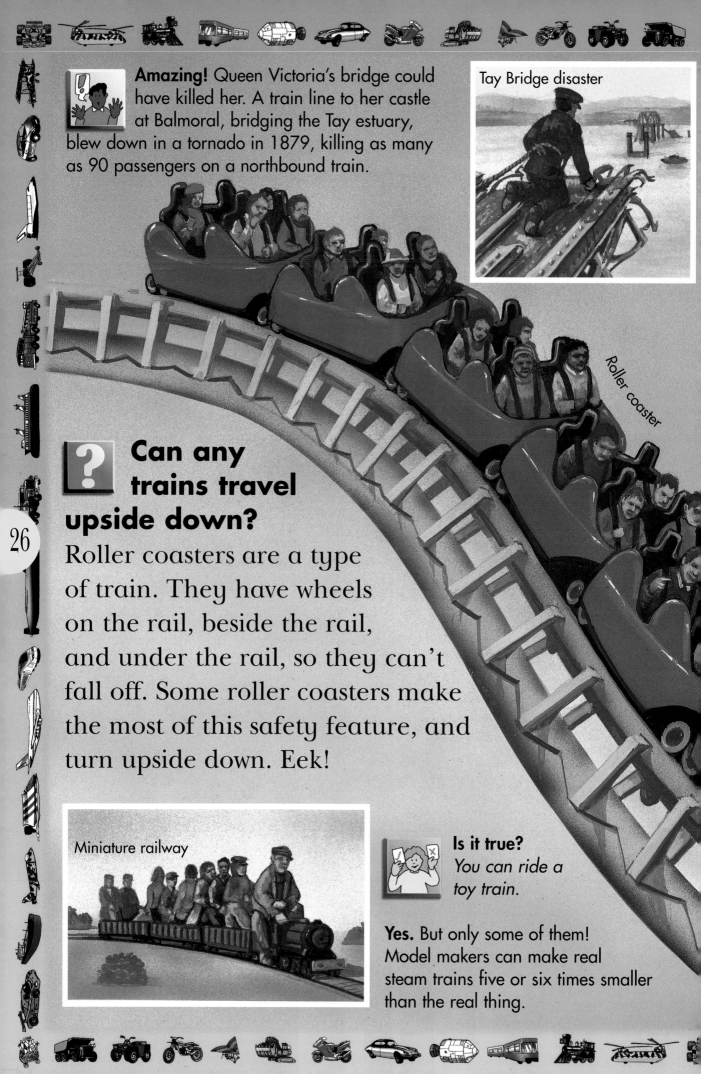

Amazing! Queen Victoria's bridge could have killed her. A train line to her castle at Balmoral, bridging the Tay estuary, blew down in a tornado in 1879, killing as many as 90 passengers on a northbound train.

Tay Bridge disaster

Roller coaster

? Can any trains travel upside down?

Roller coasters are a type of train. They have wheels on the rail, beside the rail, and under the rail, so they can't fall off. Some roller coasters make the most of this safety feature, and turn upside down. Eek!

Miniature railway

Is it true?
You can ride a toy train.

Yes. But only some of them! Model makers can make real steam trains five or six times smaller than the real thing.

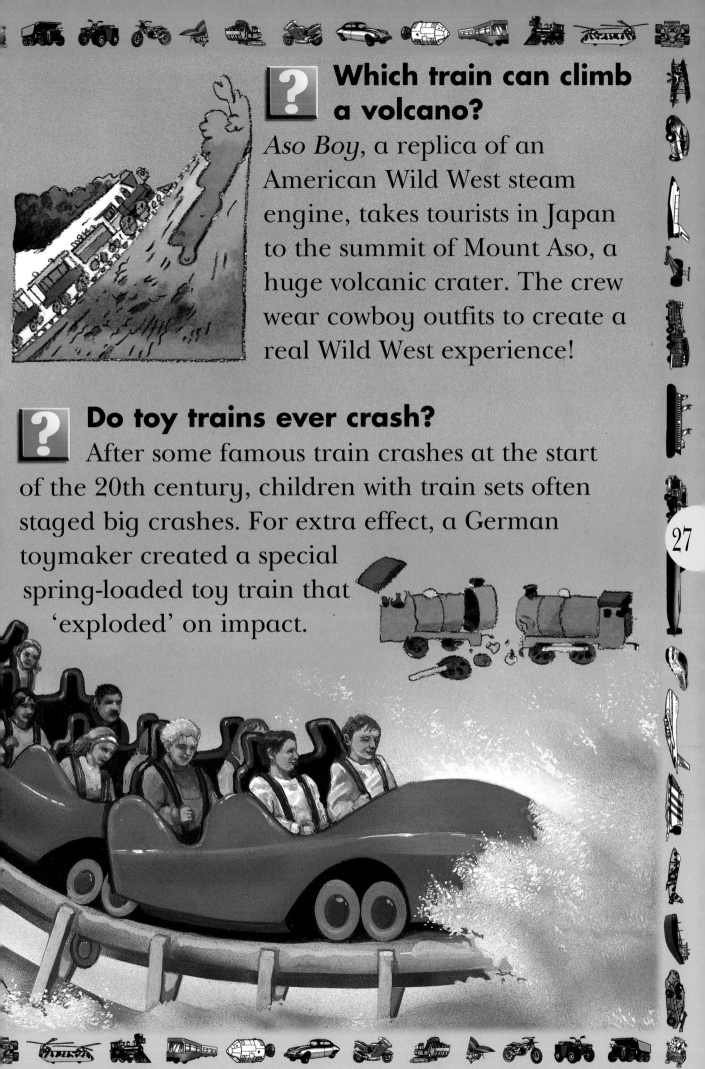

Which train can climb a volcano?

Aso Boy, a replica of an American Wild West steam engine, takes tourists in Japan to the summit of Mount Aso, a huge volcanic crater. The crew wear cowboy outfits to create a real Wild West experience!

Do toy trains ever crash?

After some famous train crashes at the start of the 20th century, children with train sets often staged big crashes. For extra effect, a German toymaker created a special spring-loaded toy train that 'exploded' on impact.

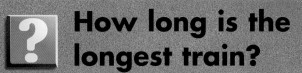

? How long is the longest train?

The longest train ever was a freight train measuring 7.3 kilometres! The longest passenger train was a measly 1.7 kilometres, but the Belgian railway couldn't find a platform long enough to park it!

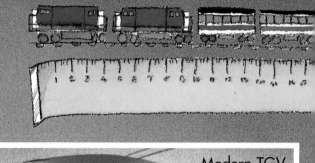

Modern TGV

Track-laying

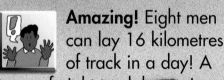

Amazing! Eight men can lay 16 kilometres of track in a day! A team of eight track-layers in America set this world record on April 18, 1869.

? Which train is fastest?

France pioneered fast trains after World War Two When Japan introduced the Shinkansen 'bullet train' in the 1960s, France responded with the TGV. An experimental TGV has reached 515 kph!

Is it true?

A train can weigh more than the Eiffel Tower.

Yes. An Australian mine train was weighed in 1996 at 72,191 tonnes – that's more than eight Eiffel Towers!

Trans-Siberian Express

? Which train travels farthest?

The once-daily service between Moscow and Vladivostock in Russia travels 9,350 kilometres, taking eight days. Known as the Trans-Siberian Express, or The Russia, the train has featured in several books and films. It is second only in fame to the Orient Express.

Which train flies?

Really fast future trains might not bother with wheels. They could ride on a cushion of air, like a hovercraft. The nose of the train squashes air underneath its belly as it jets along, and the squashed air lifts it above the ground. The *Aerotrain* already exists as an experimental vehicle.

Amazing! One sled travelled at Mach 8. An unmanned rocket vehicle on rails achieved 9,851 kph in an American experiment in 1982. On straight track, it could make the eight-day Trans-Siberian trip in less than one hour!

Aerotrain

What is a bullet train?

Japan's fastest trains, the Shinkansen, were nicknamed bullet trains because of their pointy noses – and high speed! The fastest, *Nozomi*, travels at 300 kph. With no time wasted at airports, travelling by *Nozomi* can be quicker than flying by jet!

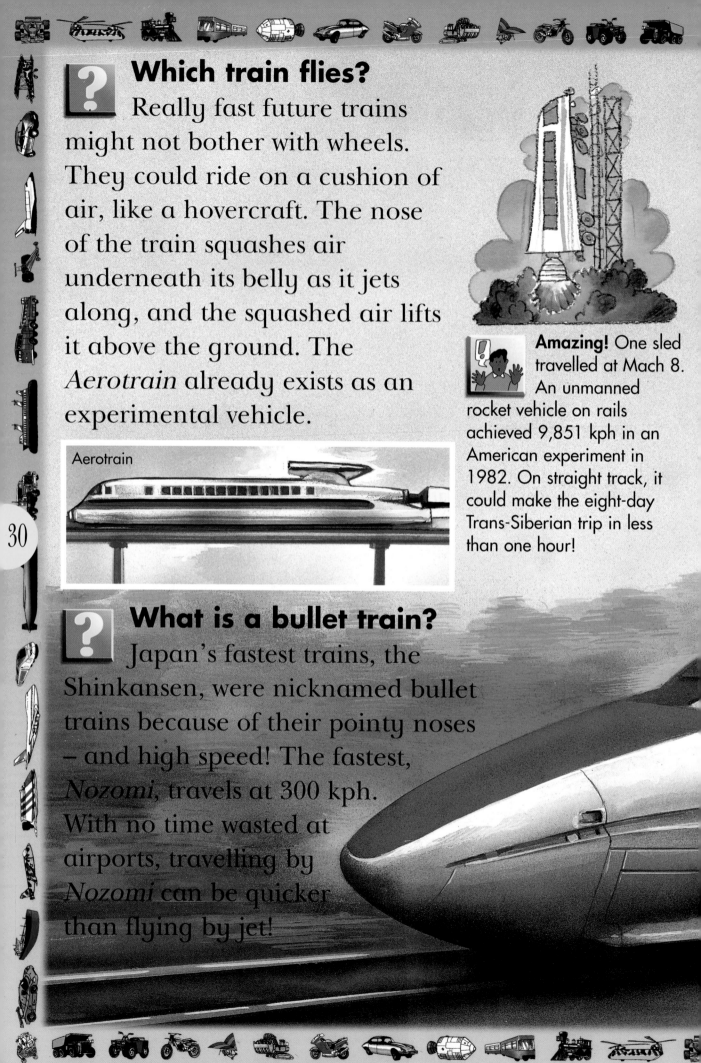

Are trains 'green'?

Trains are less harmful to the environment than most other kinds of transport. They are particularly important in cities, where underground trains, trams and monorails can reduce pollution from cars, buses and taxis. For long distance journeys, trains use much less fuel than jet aircraft.

Is it true?
Some trains run on magnets.

Yes. Germany and Japan have both tested trains that use repelling magnets to float above the track. The track doesn't wear out, and the trains can slip along at amazing speeds.

JR500 Shinkansen bullet train

31

Glossary

Air brake A network of brakes along a train which uses compressed air to squeeze the brakes closed.

Diesel engine A powerful oil-burning engine, which runs on diesel fuel.

Engineer A person who uses scientific knowledge to make useful things such as trains or bridges.

Fuel Fuel is burnt to create heat to power an engine.

Generator A machine which converts movement into electricity.

Horse-power The measurement of the strength of an engine. One horsepower equals about 750 Watts, or the power of 15 lightbulbs.

Junction A point where two or more railway tracks are joined.

Mach The measurement of the speed of sound – Mach 2 is twice the speed of sound.

Magnets Objects which attract or repel metal. In trains, very strong magnets are powered by electricity.

Pistons Sliding parts inside an engine which push the wheels around.

Platform The area in a railway station, where passengers get in and out of trains.

Pollution The mess caused by fuel-burning machines, which can be dangerous.

Trams Electric trains which run in city streets, cleaner and quieter than buses.

Index